Empires in the Middle Ages

The Holy Roman Empire

Edited by
Carolyn DeCarlo

Britannica® Educational Publishing
in association with
ROSEN
EDUCATIONAL SERVICES

Published in 2018 by Britannica Educational Publishing (a trademark of Encyclopædia Britannica, Inc.) in association with The Rosen Publishing Group, Inc. 29 East 21st Street, New York, NY 10010

Distributed exclusively by Rosen Publishing.
To see additional Britannica Educational Publishing titles, go to rosenpublishing.com.

First Edition

Britannica Educational Publishing
J.E. Luebering: Executive Director, Core Editorial
Andrea R. Field: Managing Editor, Compton's by Britannica

Rosen Publishing
Carolyn DeCarlo: Editor
Nelson Sá: Art Director
Brian Garvey: Designer
Cindy Reiman: Photography Manager
Nicole Baker: Photo Researcher

Library of Congress Cataloging-in-Publication Data

Names: DeCarlo, Carolyn, editor.
Title: The Holy Roman Empire / edited by Carolyn DeCarlo.
Description: New York : Britannica Educational Publishing, in Association with Rosen Educational Services, 2018. | Series: Empires in the Middle Ages | Audience: Grades 5-8. | Includes bibliographical references and index.
Identifiers: LCCN 2017017940| ISBN 9781680487824 (library bound : alkaline paper) | ISBN 9781680488623 (paperback : alkaline paper) | ISBN 9781680488630 (6 pack : alkaline paper)
Subjects: LCSH: Holy Roman Empire—History—Juvenile literature. | Franks—History—Juvenile literature. | Germany—History–To 1517—Juvenile literature. | Austria—History–To 1273—Juvenile literature. | Austria—History–1273-1519—Juvenile literature.
Classification: LCC DD89 .D38 2018 | DDC 943/.02—dc23
LC record available at https://lccn.loc.gov/2017017940

Manufactured in China.

Photo credits: Cover, p. 35 Imagno/Hulton Fine Art Archive/Getty Images; pp. 5, 15 © Encyclopaedia Britannica, Inc., p. 6 © Digital Vision/Getty Images; pp. 7, 41 © Photos.com/Thinkstock; p. 10 Apic/Hulton Archive/Getty Images; pp. 11, 26, 38 © Photos.com/JupiterImages; p. 13 ullstein bild/Getty Images; p. 16 Leemage/Corbis Historical/Getty Images; p. 18 © Courtesy of the Bayerisches National Museum, Munich, photograph, Foto Marburg; pp. 20–21 Fine Art/ Corbis Historical/Getty Images; p. 22 © Alexander/Fotolia; pp. 24, 29 De Agostini/Getty Images; p. 31© Courtesy of the Biblioteca Apostolica Vaticana; p. 32 © Courtesy of the Burgerbibliothek Bern, Switzerland; p. 36 Universal Images Group/Getty Images; p. 40 Universal History Archive/ Universal Images Group/Getty Images; cover and interior pages background designs Mikado767/iStock/Thinkstock (circles), Andrey_Kuzmin/Shutterstock.com (forged metal).

CONTENTS

INTRODUCTION

From Christmas Day in 800 CE until August 6, 1806, there existed in Europe a peculiar political institution called the Holy Roman Empire—though this is a bit of a misnomer. The name of the empire as it is known today did not come into general use until 1254. It has been said that this political arrangement was not holy, Roman, or an empire.

Any holiness attached to it came from the claims of the popes in their attempts to assert religious control in Europe. It was Roman to the extent that it tried to revive—without success—the political authority of the Roman Empire in the West as a counterweight to the Byzantine Empire in the East. And it was an empire in the loosest sense of the word—at no time was it able to establish unchallenged political control over the vast territories it pretended to rule. In fact, there was no central government, no unity of language, no common system of law, and no sense of common loyalty among the many states within it. And over the centuries, the empire's boundaries shifted and shrank drastically. How did this oddly named institution last for over a thousand years?

The sprawling ninth-century empire of Charlemagne covered a great part of Europe. Less than thirty years after his death, however, it was partitioned into three weak kingdoms.

The original Roman Empire ended in Italy and Western Europe in 476 CE, when the last emperor—Romulus Augustulus—was deposed. Political power passed to Constantinople (now Istanbul, Turkey), the capital of the Byzantine Empire. Theoretically, Constantinople included all of Europe in its domain. Realistically, however, this proved impossible, as barbarian kingdoms were established throughout Western Europe. The only figure in the West who had

A modern photograph of Istanbul includes the iconic Galata Tower, built by the Genoese in 1348, with the Bosphorus Strait visible in the foreground.

any claim to universal authority was the pope in Rome, but legally, he was the bishop of Rome, confirmed in his position by the Byzantine emperor.

By the eighth century, Byzantine control of Italy had vanished. The Lombard kingdom of northern Italy had driven out the emperor's representative in Ravenna in 751. There were also strong religious differences between the pope and the church in Constantinople—differences that would lead to a complete break in 1054. Confronted with this situation, the Roman popes sought political protection from the only

Pippin the Short, in a nineteenth-century chromolithograph.

people who would give it—the kings of the Franks, the strongest power north of the Alps. In 754, Frankish king Pippin the Short invaded Italy and conquered the Lombard kingdom. Two years later, Pippin assigned the former Byzantine territory around Ravenna to the pope—creating the Papal States of Italy, which would endure until the unification of Italy in the nineteenth century.

The close cooperation between popes and the Frankish kings had far-reaching consequences. It laid the basis for centuries of conflict between emperors and popes over who had the supreme authority in Europe. According to the popes, the empire was the political arm of the church. The emperors, however, saw themselves as directly responsible to God—and they relied solely on conquest and control for their power.

CHAPTER 1

CHARLEMAGNE'S EMPIRE

There is little doubt that the popes hoped to become the successors of the emperors in the West. Since this was politically impossible, the next best solution was to assert religious control by means of political institutions. On December 25, 800, Pope Leo III crowned Charlemagne emperor during a service at St. Peter's Basilica in Rome. It had been expected that the pope would consecrate Charlemagne's son as king, but as Charlemagne himself rose from prayer, Leo placed a crown on his head, and the assembled Romans acclaimed him as emperor.

But the one thousand years of tumult in store for the Holy Roman Empire was almost cut to a fraction of that length. In 806, Charlemagne made arrangements to divide his territories among his three sons. One has to wonder whether the Holy Roman Empire would have survived even past Charlemagne's lifetime if two of the emperor's sons had not died before him, leaving

Pope Leo III crowns Charlemagne emperor on Christmas Day in 800.

the undivided inheritance to his third son, Louis I the Pious.

A PAPAL AGENDA

It seems clear that Charlemagne's coronation was the work of the papacy, not of the Frankish king, who is said to have been surprised and angry at it. The immediate beneficiary of the coronation was the pope, whose position in the empire was secured. Charlemagne was left to face the momentous consequences and to try to

Charlemagne became king of the Franks in 768 CE.

CHARLEMAGNE THE MAN

The man now known as Charlemagne became king of the Franks in 768. His name means "Charles the Great." Charlemagne belonged to the Carolingians, a particularly powerful branch of the Franks. The Franks, for whom France is named, were a Germanic-speaking people. Within a few decades, his conquests had united almost all the Christian lands of western Europe into one state, which became known as the Holy Roman Empire.

Charlemagne had deep sympathy for the peasants and believed that government should be for the benefit of the governed. When he came to the throne, various local governors, called counts, had become lax and oppressive. To reform them, he expanded the work of investigators, called *missi dominici*. He prescribed their duties in documents called capitularies and sent them out in teams of two—a churchman and a noble. They rode to all parts of the realm, inspecting government, administering justice, and reawakening all citizens to their civil and religious duties. Twice a year, Charlemagne summoned the chief men of the empire to discuss its affairs. In all problems, he was the final arbiter—even in church issues—and he largely unified church and state.

Charlemagne was a tireless reformer who tried to improve his people's lot in many ways. He set up money standards to encourage commerce, tried to build a Rhine-Danube canal, and urged better farming methods. He especially worked to spread education and Christianity in every class of people. He built the cathedral at Aachen, his capital in western Germany. He also revived the Palace School. He set up other schools, opening them to peasant boys as well as nobles.

Charlemagne never stopped studying. He brought an English monk, Alcuin, and other scholars to his court. He learned to read Latin and some Greek but never mastered writing. At meals, instead of having jesters perform, he listened to men reading from learned works. To revive church music, Charlemagne had monks sent from Rome to train his Frankish singers. To restore some appreciation of art, he brought valuable pieces from Italy.

Aachen Cathedral, located in Aachen, Germany, contains the tomb of the emperor Charlemagne.

gain recognition from Constantinople, without which his title was legally invalid.

In fact, the act itself was illegal, because popes never had the right to crown emperors. The crowning did nothing positive for Charlemagne—he was, as before, king of the Franks and Lombards and the most powerful monarch in Europe. The main practical outcome of Leo's act was to complete the separation between East and West. Admittedly, this was not Charlemagne's intent. He sought to reunite the two by offering marriage to Byzantine Empress Irene. Unfortunately, revolution in Constantinople and the deposition of Irene in 802 brought that plan to a halt.

The coronation of Charlemagne was an extralegal and therefore revolutionary proceeding. The pope had no right to make him emperor. Nor did the coronation create a new western empire by the side of the existing eastern empire. A usurper in the eyes of the Byzantines, Charlemagne's coronation thereby represented a rivalry with Constantinople—a rivalry in which neither side had a real advantage.

CONSEQUENCES OF THE CORONATION

In 812, after unsuccessful war and wearisome negotiation, the Byzantine emperor Michael I recognized Charlemagne's imperial title. It was still a personal title, and Charlemagne was recognized merely as emperor, not as emperor of the Romans; in other words, the emperor in Constantinople maintained his claim to be the only true successor to the Roman Caesars. Moreover, the recognition was grudgingly given, and later, when Byzantium was stronger and the Carolingians weaker, Michael's successors refused to extend

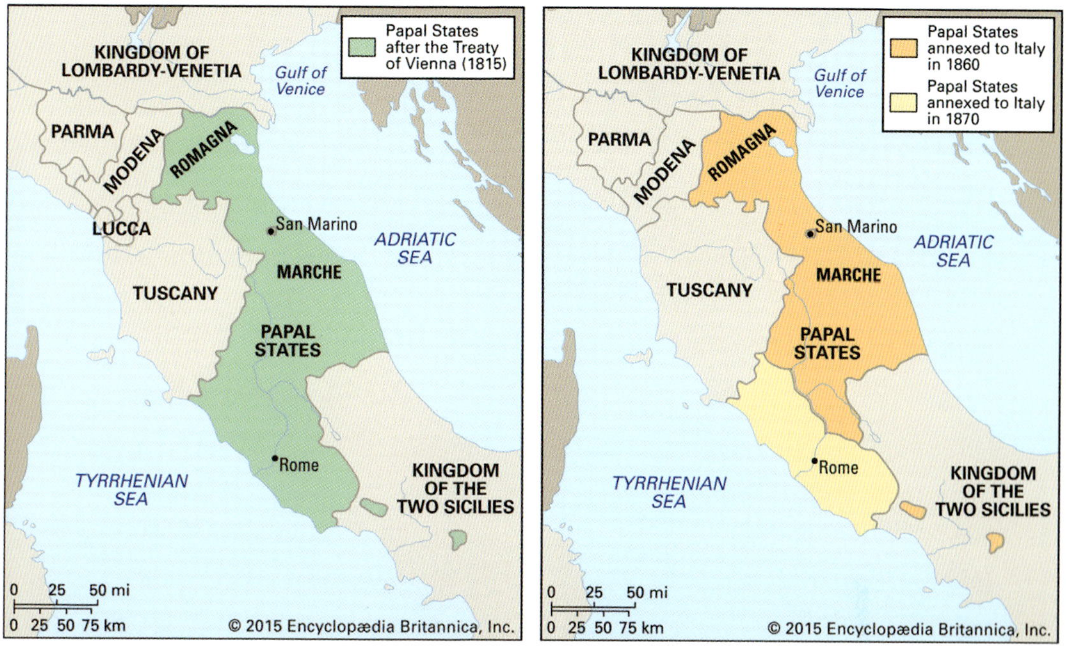

The Papal States in 1815 *(left)* and at their annexation by Italy in 1870.

it automatically to Charlemagne's successors. This rivalry with Constantinople remained an important factor in imperial history until at least 1204.

Charlemagne's coronation involved the new emperor and his successors in the political pretensions of the papacy. The relationship between the papacy and the Frankish rulers, close for nearly fifty years before 800, was intensified when the Roman See became the first metropolitan church of Charlemagne's dominions. Religious emperors and their ecclesiastical advisers would forevermore recognize the promotion of Christian unity as the main function

TRANSFERENCE OF POWER: A DIFFERENT STYLE

In 813, after his agreement with Michael I, Charlemagne decided to bestow the imperial crown on his only surviving son, Louis. Wishing to exclude the papacy from any part in the bestowal, he framed his actions accordingly. The ceremony took place in an imperial chapel at Aachen, rather than in Rome; the pope was not present; the constitutive act was at the approval of the gathered Frankish nobility; and Louis either received the crown from his father or took it with his own hands from the altar.

The contrast with the Roman ceremony of 800 was deliberate. Henceforward, the conflict between the two contrary views or theories of the empire—the papal and the Frankish—was to be a dominant theme.

This French miniature dating to the fifteenth century depicts the construction of the palace of Aachen (Aix-la-Chapelle), with Charlemagne overseeing the build.

attached to their imperial duty. Furthermore, the fact that the pope had crowned Charlemagne emperor—rightfully or not—could not but impress. It was Pope Leo III who had taken the initiative and transferred the empire from the Greeks to the Germans. His successors would argue that they could therefore transfer it elsewhere if they so wished.

CHARLEMAGNE'S SUCCESSORS

As it turns out, Louis I the Pious was in every way different from his father, Charlemagne. For Louis, the word "empire" was the unifying idea holding together his various dominions. In 817, he made his eldest son, Lothar I, emperor with him under the power of the *Ordinatio imperii* (imperial dignity). Unfortunately, he aroused the conservative opposition of the Frankish nobility, involving the Frankish lands in civil war. This internal dissension ultimately helped the papacy by increasing its influence: by 816, the pope had persuaded Louis to be re-crowned, repairing the defect of his father's ceremony in Aachen. And though Lothar had been made emperor without papal intervention in 817 as Louis had been in 813, Louis's son also saw fit to strengthen his title by being crowned in Rome in 823.

Thus the empire, instead of remaining loyal to the Frankish kingship, was drawn back into the papal sphere. Lothar's son Louis II was crowned by the pope in 850, his uncle Charles II the Bald was emperor from

The seal of Charles III the Fat, ca. ninth century.

875 to 877, and Charles III the Fat was crowned emperor in 881. But the imperial title, without power to support it, was merely a name—and with the dislocation of the Carolingian realm, culminating in the deposition of Charles the Fat by the East Frankish magnates in 887, its decline was rapid.

From 888 France, Germany, and Italy were separate states (though not unified nations by any means). A succession of emperors, mostly nominees of the popes, followed Charles. But such men were of little use to the papacy, and the papacy in its current state was of little use to them. With the death of the last of them in 924, the powerful Roman family of the Crescentii, determined to keep authority in its own hands, abolished the title of emperor in Italy—at least for a time.

CHAPTER 2

A GERMANIC RULE

The imperial title may have died temporarily in Italy, but it persisted north of the Alps. Yet it was a notion of empire that had nothing to do with Rome or even the papacy. The Frankish tradition of empire looked back to Charlemagne, reflecting a notion of unity amid the divisions of the dwindling ninth century. It was also seen as the expression of power and hegemony, and of rule—as Charlemagne had ruled—over a number of different countries.

TWO FRANKISH KINGDOMS: EAST AND WEST

By the middle of the tenth century, there were two Frankish kingdoms—East and West. The West Kingdom was composed largely of today's France. The East Frankish Kingdom was Germanic. The first Saxon king of Germany, Henry I, was acclaimed emperor because

A hand-colored map, dating to 1657 CE, depicting the empire of Charlemagne.

of his victory over the Hungarians in 933. Indeed, the successor-states that are called France and Germany remained Frankish—the West Frankish and the East Frankish kingdoms. And in the East Frankish lands, the kings were Saxon.

From this time, the Holy Roman Empire was to be basically Germanic, though it maintained pretensions of rule over greater territory, including Italy. Otto I was the first of the Saxon kings powerful enough to assert control over Germany and Italy. Otto succeeded to the East Frankish throne in 936 as the true heir of Charlemagne. He spread Christianity among the Slavic Wends by making churchmen his ministers and establishing missionary districts on the Elbe River. In 951, Otto descended on Italy, married the late king's widow, and forced the new king to hold his kingdom as a vassal of the German crown.

Otto I was crowned emperor by Pope John XII in 962. By Otto's time the import of that title scarcely extended beyond protection or "advocacy" of the Roman church. So, too, the territorial extent of the empire had decreased. Although he held the title, Otto I made no pretense of governing the West Frankish lands. Likewise, he did not claim the title of Roman emperor. From his reign, the empire was to be a union of German states and northern Italy. His successors certainly did not seek to exercise world dominion, nor did they seek to challenge the Byzantine emperors in their rule over the empire of the East.

Nevertheless, the problem of the relations of the two empires reasserted itself, for the Byzantine Empire

GREAT REFORMERS: THE ABBOTS OF CLUNY

The octagonal belfry tower and smaller belfry of the surviving south transept of the abbey church of St. Peter and St. Paul at Cluny, France, constructed 1088–1130.

The revival of imperial power in Germany had a lasting influence on the development of the Roman church, as would the foundation of the reformed monastery of Cluny in Burgundy in 909. The empire had the support of the abbots of Cluny—some of the greatest reformers of the age—who looked to the emperor rather than to the pope as the effective head of Latin Christendom. Indeed, the first stirrings of the great reform movement that transformed the church in the eleventh century are thought to have taken place at Cluny.

Established by Duke William I the Pious of Aquitaine, Cluny rose to prominence under the direction of abbots Odo, Odilo, and Hugh, who were the spiritual leaders of their age. From its beginning, Cluny enjoyed close ties with Rome because William had placed the monastery under the protection of St. Peter, St. Paul, and the pope. William also ensured Cluny's independence by forbidding any secular or religious authority from interfering in its affairs. Cluny developed a reputation as the highest form of religious life—indeed, as a paradise on earth—and its abbots spread Cluniac practices by reforming other monasteries.

Cluniac monks lived strictly canonical lives, opposing simony and clerical unchastity. They also participated in an elaborate liturgical routine, singing the monastic hours (liturgical or devotional services for use at certain hours of the day, according to the monastic daily schedule) and offering prayers for the dead and the monastery's numerous benefactors. Cluny was not the only reformed house to support the Holy Roman Empire, but it was the greatest, and the ideals it embodied set an important precedent.

had made rapid recovery and was preparing to embark on expansion and reconquest. Fears of Byzantine interference in Roman politics and conflicting claims in southern Italy soon brought the two powers into rivalry, and the conflict proved to be the catalyst for a major development—the Romanization of the western empire.

This miniature from a tenth-century Italian manuscript shows Otto I being crowned by the Virgin Mary.

THE OTTONIAN EMPIRE

Whereas Otto I shied away from the Roman title, Otto II claimed the title of Roman emperor to proclaim his rivalry with the emperor at Constantinople. Otto III (ruled 983–1002) made Rome his capital. From this, it was only a short step to describing the empire itself as the Roman Empire, a change which occurred in Conrad II's reign (1024–39; crowned 1027). It is noteworthy, however, that these formal changes were the result not of claims to the heritage of ancient Rome or of universal pretensions but simply of rivalry with Byzantium.

Otto III felt himself to be the political power by which Christian domination would spread throughout Europe. The son of a Greek princess, instilled with Byzantine traditions, Otto III drew on Roman, Carolingian, and Christian strands to form a new synthesis combining the heterogeneous elements in the imperial idea. Rome was to be his capital, the pope his lieutenant in the spread of Christian dominion. Distance alone made unified imperial rule over Germany and Italy impossible. Otto himself lost Rome shortly before his death. What did survive—as the characteristic feature of the empire from Otto I to Henry III—was the close subordination of pope to emperor.

Popes were subject to Otto III and his successors down to Henry III (1039–56). And many were deposed and nominated under their rule. This was not the result of oppression or force but rather the fulfillment

Otto III was crowned Holy Roman Emperor in 996. He had been the German king since 983.

of the emperor's supreme duty—to watch over the welfare of the church. The iconography of the time shows the emperor, not the pope, as the representative of St. Peter and often standing alone as God's vicar on earth. This period from 962 to 1046 saw the empire at its zenith. No other kingdom of Europe was its match.

CHAPTER 3

REASSERTION OF PAPAL POWER

From the middle of the eleventh century, effective rule over Germany and Italy together became unviable. One cause was the rapid progress of European economic recovery, which brought shifts of power detrimental to Germany. More immediately important was the revival of the papacy. For more than two hundred years after Henry III's death in 1056, the popes maintained their political comeback. During this period, some very strong-minded individuals were elected pope. Among them, Gregory VII and Innocent III were the most notable; they wasted no time in refuting the pretensions of the emperors to control the church.

The challenge thrown out by Gregory VII in his statement of papal right forced the emperors to seek new foundations for their position. Pope Gregory's great opponent, the emperor Henry IV, asserted the traditional rights of his father. His successors in the

THE INVESTITURE CONTROVERSY

The Investiture Controversy brought matters to a head. At issue was the question of whether political figures such as emperors and kings had the right to appoint bishops and heads of monasteries and to invest them with the symbols of their office. At the heart of the issue was the place of the emperor in Christian society, especially his relationship with the papacy. Pope Gregory VII (pope 1073–85) initiated the controversy in 1076 by stating that it was his sole right to appoint bishops and other church officials. A compromise was reached in 1122 between Pope Calixtus II and Emperor Henry V that reserved for the pope all spiritual rights in the appointment of bishops and abbots, who would, however, swear an oath of loyalty and pay homage to the emperor before taking office. This agreement largely settled the controversy, but future popes revived the issue as they saw fit.

Henry IV asks for Pope Gregory VII and Matilda of Canossa's forgiveness at the Audience of Canossa in 1077. The Holy Roman Emperor was excommunicated twice by Pope Gregory VII, first in 1076 and again in 1080.

twelfth century shifted their ground. To counter the arguments of church lawyers they grasped the weapons provided by the revival of Roman law. A new and more exalted conception of the empire was the result.

THE HOHENSTAUFEN DYNASTY

The era of the Hohenstaufen emperors (1138–1254, except for the years 1198–1214) was a time of almost unceasing conflict between popes and emperors. The greatest of these, Frederick I Barbarossa—a strong figure in the Crusades—added the word *sacrum* (meaning "holy") to the name of his empire to balance the claims of the Holy Church. He emphasized continuity with the past, going back to the days of Charlemagne. For this reason, he chose to see Charlemagne canonized by Paschal III in 1165—asserting his right as Charlemagne's successor. His rights as emperor, he determined, were not based on the deed of Leo III but on the territorial conquest of the Franks.

Unlike earlier emperors, who had based their position on their special relation with the church, the Hohenstaufen emperors emphasized its secular foundations. Lawyers for the emperors argued against the popes, saying that "he who is chosen by the election of the princes alone is the true emperor." The emperors were generally chosen by this time through an election held by German princes.

FREDERICK I BARBAROSSA

Frederick, the nephew of the German king Conrad III, invaded Italy in 1154 and was crowned emperor at Rome in 1155. His beard led the Italians to give him the nickname Barbarossa (Red Beard). His efforts in Italy were, in the long run, unsuccessful. Times had changed since Charlemagne had founded the empire in 800. The pope played a much stronger role in European affairs, and a number of powerful city-states had grown up in northern Italy. Several of the city-states formed a group called the Lombard League to oppose Frederick. The League's army defeated him at the battle of Legnano in 1176. The cities then became almost completely independent.

As a young man, Frederick had accompanied Conrad III on the Second Crusade to the Holy Land. In 1189 Frederick called for a Third Crusade to free Jerusalem from the Muslims. On the trek through Asia Minor with his army, he drowned in the Saleph River in 1190.

Frederick I is depicted as a Crusader, with a cross on the breast of his tunic. At right, a man dedicates to Frederick a copy of the *History of the First Crusade* by Robert of St. Remy. The artwork is a miniature from a manuscript in the Vatican Library.

POPES AND CONFLICT

The conflicts with the popes and the desire to restore the territorial basis of imperial power, which the Investiture Controversy had shattered, drew the Hohenstaufen emperors more and more into Italian politics. The temptation to control Italy, and thus Rome, was persistent. Frederick's son, Henry VI, married the heiress to Sicily, and his inheritance of the Norman kingdom of southern Italy and Sicily was used to restore imperial power in Italy. It was a grandiose policy but overstrained. The papacy, fearing that Rome would be engulfed, reacted vigorously to this threat.

The Hohenstaufen Holy Roman Emperor Henry VI is portrayed in a miniature from a manuscript in the Burgerbibliothek in Bern, Switzerland.

The popes found allies in their opposition to the emperors. Pope Innocent III, profiting from German dissensions after the early death of Henry VI, played upon the German factions. Henry VI's son Frederick II made concessions to the German princes in order to ensure their support for his Italian policy, but in vain. In spite of some victories on the battlefield, Frederick II was excommunicated in 1239 and deposed in 1245. By the time of his death in 1250, Frederick had lost much of central Italy.

In Germany, a long interregnum (1250–1273) brought down the imperial structure. In Italy, to ensure that there could be no restoration, the papacy called in Charles of Anjou—from the French royal house—who conquered the south and became King Charles I of Naples and Sicily.

CHAPTER 4

THE HOUSE OF HAPSBURG

The empire was able to maintain itself north of the Alps in Germany for several centuries past 1250 as little more than a coalition of German states, each with its own ruler. When Rudolf I of the House of Hapsburg became German king in 1273, it was as the head of a federation of German princes. He abandoned all claims to the center and south of Italy and retained only nominal titles in the north, which remained entangled in Hapsburg domination until after World War I.

AN EMPIRE, OF SORTS

Though it continued, the title of emperor usually did not have the support of personal crowning by a pope or papal legate. For a century after Frederick II's death the only "true" emperor was Henry VII, who was crowned in Rome in 1312 by representatives of

A stained glass window in St. Stephen's Cathedral, Vienna, ca. 1390, depicts King Rudolf I of Hapsburg (1218–1291).

the Avignon pope. After Henry VII, only four emperors were crowned by a pope or his delegate: Charles IV (reigned 1355–78); Sigismund (1410–37); Frederick III (1440–93); and Charles V (1519–56).

By the end of the Middle Ages, any hope of reviving anything like a real empire in Europe had become impossible. France and Spain were the most powerful kingdoms in Europe. Both were contending for control of the continent. The weak and disunited German states were in no position to establish any kind of control, even within their own boundaries—Germany did not become united until 1870. Charles IV, therefore, set out to make the empire a solely German institution. In an agreement

The Council of Constance brought the Holy Roman Emperor Sigismund into contact with King Ferdinand I of Aragon and his queen, as they met as members of the council to elect Pope Martin V in 1417 and end the Great Western Schism.

with Pope Clement V, he abandoned Italy entirely. He travelled to Rome only for his coronation on April 5, 1355, then set about refashioning the empire into the Holy Roman Empire of the German Nation.

From that point, the empire essentially became part of the history of Germany. It is true that memories of an imperial past continued to have an influence on German thinking and that in the Hapsburg lands there was a sense of belonging to a multinational empire. A few emperors, notably Charles V in the sixteenth century, entertained a larger vision of power.

Though Charles V was also the king of Spain, there was no way for him to unite his Spanish and Austrian possessions with Germany as long as France stood in the way. When Charles, opening the Diet of Worms in 1521, declared that "the empire from of old

THE DIET OF WORMS

At a meeting of the Diet (assembly) of the Holy Roman Empire held at Worms, Germany, in 1521, the German monk Martin Luther defended the principles of the Reformation. Luther had already been excommunicated by Pope Leo X, but Emperor Charles V granted him safe conduct to a hearing at the Diet. On April 17, 1521, Luther refused to recant his views. Disorder broke out, the emperor adjourned the proceedings, and Luther was obliged to

(Continued on the next page)

(Continued from the previous page)

go into hiding. In May, the Diet issued the Edict of Worms, declaring Luther an outlaw and a heretic and banning his writings.

Luther's efforts to reform the Roman Catholic Church ultimately led to the establishment of Protestant forms of Christianity, including Lutheranism. Emperor Charles V defeated a group of Protestant princes at Mühlberg in eastern Germany in April 1547. Nevertheless, only eight years later he was forced to allow the Peace of Augsburg, which acknowledged the legitimacy of Lutheranism within the Holy Roman Empire.

Woodcut of Pope Leo X supervising the burning of Martin Luther's books after the Diet of Worms in 1521.

had not many masters, but one, and it is our intention to be that one," he was shutting his eyes to the realities. The size of his dominions was imposing, but they were a weak collection of territories. And though Charles championed the Roman Catholic Church against the Reformation, his empire was neither in spirit nor in fact a revival of the medieval empire.

FROM DIVISION TO RESIGNATION

The sixteenth-century Reformation in the church further divided the weak empire. Germany was split into two religious camps, and the emperor became little more than the head of a religious faction. The electors—the real heads of the German states—were established by virtue of championing either Roman Catholicism or Lutheranism.

Likewise, the Thirty Years' War (1618–48), originally a religious conflict, devastated Germany and further weakened what little reality the empire had left. No emperor afterward ever tried to establish a central authority. Yet, even at the end, the empire had loyal adherents, particularly among the small knights and noblemen of western Germany, who regarded it as their safeguard against princely absolutism. Its loose structure still suited to some degree the cosmopolitan spirit of the eighteenth century.

The end came with Napoleon Bonaparte. For several centuries, France had been intending to annex at

In this illustration from the *Grandes Chroniques de France*, Charles IV, the first king of Bohemia to be named a Holy Roman emperor, receives gifts from the people of Paris with his son, the future Wenceslas IV, on a visit to France.

least the fringes of the empire. It had never happened. Napoleon, posing as the "new Charlemagne," carried his wars eastward—resolving to terminate the reign of Emperor Francis II (later Francis I of Austria). The emperor saw what was coming, and he resigned his imperial title on August 6, 1806. From this point, the empire ceased to exist as a political reality, persisting only as an ideological background to the creation of the Second Reich, or German Empire, in 1871 and Adolf Hitler's Third Reich in the 1930s. Thus, the Holy Roman Empire came to an official end with Francis II in 1806, after a history of a thousand years.

Napoleon Bonaparte wears his imperial robes upon his coronation as emperor of France in 1804.

GLOSSARY

absolutism A political theory that total power should be vested in one or more rulers.

annex To incorporate a country or other territory within the domain of a state.

barbarian Of or relating to a land, culture, or people alien and usually believed to be inferior to another land, culture, or people; lacking refinement, learning, or artistic or literary culture.

catalyst An agent that provokes or speeds significant change or action.

chastity The quality or state of being chaste, such as abstention from all or unlawful sexual intercourse.

coronation The act or occasion of crowning.

cosmopolitan Having people from many different parts of the world.

depose To remove from a throne or other high position.

diet A formal deliberative assembly of princes or estates; an imperial council.

ecclesiastical Of or relating to a church, especially as an established institution.

extralegal Not regulated or sanctioned by law.

hegemony The social, cultural, ideological, or economic influence exerted by a dominant group.

heterogeneous Consisting of dissimilar or diverse ingredients or constituents.

ideological Relating to or concerned with ideas.

imperial Of, relating to, befitting, or suggestive of an empire or an emperor.

interregnum The time during which a throne is vacant between two successive reigns or regimes.

kingdom A country whose ruler is a king or queen.

misnomer Use of a wrong or inappropriate name.

papal Of or relating to a pope or to the Roman Catholic Church.

revival An act or instance of reviving, or the state of being revived, specifically to do with a period of renewed religious interest.

secular Of or relating to the worldly or temporal concerns; not outwardly or specifically religious.

simony The buying or selling of a church office or position of honor.

usurp To seize and hold (as office, place, or powers) in possession by force or without right.

vassal One in a subservient or subordinate position; a person under the protection of a feudal lord to whom he has vowed homage and fealty.

FOR FURTHER READING

Aston, Florence. *Stories from German History*. Brookfield, WI: First Rate Publishers, 2015.

Bhote, Temina. *Charlemagne: The Life and Times of an Early Medieval Emperor*. New York, NY: Rosen Publishing, 2005.

Cresswell, Julia. *Charlemagne and the Paladins* (Myths and Legends). Oxford, UK: Osprey Publishing, 2014.

Freed, John. *Frederick Barbarossa: A Prince and the Myth*. New Haven, CT: Yale UP, 2016.

Gagne, Tammy. *Charlemagne* (Jr. Biographies from Ancient Civilization). Hallandale, FL: Mitchell Lane Publishers, 2017.

Hodge, Susie. *Medieval Europe.* Milwaukee, WI: Gareth Stevens, 2005.

Judson, Pieter M. *The Habsburg Empire: A New History*. Cambridge, MA: Belknap Press, 2016.

Schmidt, Ferdinand. *The Story of Charlemagne*. Trans. George Upton. San Diego, CA: Didactic Press, 2013.

Wickham, Chris. *Medieval Europe*. New Haven, CT: Yale UP, 2016.

Wilson, Peter H. *Heart of Europe: A History of the Holy Roman Empire*. Cambridge, MA: Belknap Press, 2016.

WEBSITES

Because of the changing nature of internet links, Rosen Publishing has developed an online list of websites related to the subject of this book. This site is updated regularly. Please use this link to access this list:

http://www.rosenlinks.com/EIMA/Roman

INDEX

G

H

I

L

M

N

O

P